German Literary History for Beginners

An exciting and entertaining journey through German literature from the Middle Ages to the present day

Christian Möhlenkamp

CONTENT

What you can expect in this book......1

German literary history......4

  Middle Ages......5

  Baroque...... 10

  Enlightenment & Sturm und Drang 18

  Classic 22

  Romanticism 26

  Realism/Naturalism...... 31

  Modern 35

  Literature of the Weimar Republic...... 41

  Exile literature...... 46

  Contemporary Literature 51

German Poets, German Thinkers: Three Examples 56

  Friedrich Schiller 57

  Rainer Maria Rilke...... 61

  Daniel Kehlmann 65

From the Roots into the Future - An Outlook......69

What you can expect in this book

This book is intended for readers who are looking for an introduction to the confusing diversity of German literature. The chronological order chosen is best suited for this purpose because, in contrast to topic- or genre-oriented ordering procedures, it shows a genesis and traces the genealogy of German literature. The fact that Goethe's novel *Wilhelm Meisters Lehrjahre* would most likely have looked completely different without Hans Jakob Christoffel von Grimmelshausen's

Simplicissimus can be shown most easily and effectively in the context of a chronologically presented journey through time. And this is only one of many examples, especially in the field of poetry, many more could be found.

One could thus specify: The book is addressed to readers who want to embark on the long and exciting journey through the world of words, as heroes of their own development story, so to speak, in the course of which they gain a better and better overview and finally reach a point where it is easier for them to choose from the abundance of works those that really interest them.

The authors presented as examples in the second part can serve as an appetizer; they can certainly be considered representative of German literature. Schiller's works will appeal above all to those who are enthusiastic about perfectly formed, thematically complex and linguistically beautiful plays or ballads of almost epic proportions, while Rilke's texts are more likely to appeal to you if you like metrically shaped poems or cycles of poems that work with numerous intertextual and intercultural references, or if you are interested in sensitive, inward-looking literature such as *The Notes of Malte Laurids Brigge* and *Letters to a Young Poet*. The bridge to the present is then built with Daniel Kehlmann, whose novels have achieved worldwide success and are proof that the German-speaking world is also intensively engaged with the literatures of other cultural regions.

"He who knows how to read holds the key to great deeds, to undreamed-of possibilities," Aldous Huxley once said. This book aims to open up some of these possibilities for you.

German literary history

From the *Merseburg Spells* to complex postmodern works such as Slata Roschal's *153 Forms of Non-Being,* published in 2022: German literature has a lot to offer, and this amount is to be traversed piece by piece, it is to be prepared for a word hike that is about endurance and not speed.

This book, due to its length, is a parforceride through German literary history, but it can serve as a first point of reference and guide. Beginning with the archaic early medieval traditions, it will trace an arc through the courtly literary tradition of the High Middle Ages and the Baroque, the unleashing texts of the Enlightenment, the intensity of the Sturm und Drang, and the diversity of the literary 19th and early 20th centuries to the present.

MIDDLE AGES

> "bên zi bêna, bluot zi bluoda,
> lid zi geliden, sôse gelîmida sîn."

This is perhaps the most famous passage from the *Merseburg Magic Sayings, which are* one of the few Old High German language testimonies that have survived. If one translates the seemingly foreign word formations into modern German, one obtains the following:

> "Leg to leg, blood to blood,
> limb to limb, how glued they shall be!"

This translation from a Prague anthology of German poetry makes it clear how far language has moved in the meantime, what distance there is between us and a text that originated before the year 1000. The two spells, named after their place of discovery in an ecclesiastical library in Merseburg, were intended for practical use; the second, for example, from which the last lines are quoted here, was intended to be used to ask the gods to heal a horse. The Germanic tradition plays a major role here; pantheistic tendencies in particular were still widespread despite Christianization.

The unclear history of the transmission of the spells, their uncertain origin, even the ambiguity about the dialectal language area from which they originate: All this exemplifies the problems that medieval studies, the science of medieval texts, has to deal with. Even from the heyday of high medieval literature, which encompasses the 13th and 14th centuries, only a few manuscripts have survived, and in these there are often duplications, so that it is not uncommon to find four or five different versions of one and the same text, which brings with it the task of editing them appropriately.

The further one advances in time, the more diverse the selection of surviving texts becomes. It would be impossible to break down and explain all the different genres and categories, so by way of example, we will focus on two genres that are of immense importance to German literature: first, the heroic epic (or heroic poetry), and second, minnesong.

In contrast to the courtly epic of chivalry, the German heroic epic is mostly based on Germanic sagas and traditions. These were taken up in a fixed form and told in verse; only details deviated from the traditional story, for example when a different moral was desired. Constitutive for the understanding of the author in the Middle Ages is anyway that he was granted little freedom and that the most recognition was given to those who best imitated the great, canonized masters.

The classic epic par excellence is the *Nibelungenlied*, which in its present form goes back to a Middle High German manuscript from the 13th century. The material, however, is considerably older and, in keeping with genre conventions, is taken from the oral narrative tradition. The extensive work about Kriemhild of Burgundy and the dragon-slayer Siegfried is of enormous cultural value not only because of Richard Wagner's opera adaptation, but also its influence on the emergence of a German national feeling - with all its fatal consequences - shows what formative influence this literary milestone has left behind.

However, the culture of the High Middle Ages was shaped not only by the more popular epic poetry, but also by courtly poetry bound to narrow conventions and ideas, especially minnesong. In addition to the so-called high minne, in which a noble lady was sung to and praised and fixed forms such as the song of praise or lament predominated, there was also the low minne, which was more concerned with conveying actual feelings than the strict specifications of the high minne would have allowed. On the other hand, low minne was also strongly oriented toward courtly models, as the perfectly formed hybridity of the poems of Walther von der Vogelweide shows.

One of the most famous minnesongs is found in a letter from a lady to a magister; it is an elaborate imitation of popular poetry, reproduced below in the original:

<blockquote>
"You are mine, I am yours. you must be sure of that.

you are chosen

in my heart,

"the sluzzelîn is lost:

You must always be in it."
</blockquote>

Poems like this show why reading medieval texts is worthwhile: because the great emotions hardly change over the centuries, because they are negotiated anew in every epoch, and because the texts dealing with them thus remain timeless.

With the Reformation and the burgeoning of humanism, with new forms of art and expression, and with Johannes Gutenberg's invention of the printing press, a new era is ushered in, the Renaissance, which completely changes the way society sees itself. At its end, confronted with drastic abysses, stands the Baroque.

BAROQUE

On May 23, 1618, two royal governors and a secretary were thrown out of the window of Prague Castle. This marked the beginning of the Thirty Years' War, which took place mainly in the territory of the Holy Roman Empire of the German Nation and did not end until the Peace of Westphalia in 1648. For Baroque literature, this was a permanently present background against which the change of literary language from Latin to German took place. Poets such as Paul Fleming, Andreas Gryphius, Martin Opitz, and Christian Hoffmann von Hoffmannswaldau, however, still stood strongly in the tradition of the Latin poetic elite of the generations before them and made less reference to the German-language literary tradition, which in the decades before had been found more in the vernacular.

Essential and formative for Baroque poetry was the first German poetics, the *Book of German Poetry from* 1624, written by Martin Opitz. In it, he attempts to establish the independence of German as a literary language and to contrast it with the Romance languages, especially French, which were perceived as superior. Opitz takes from Tacitus' descriptions of the Germanic peoples in his *Germania the* ascribed positive qualities of bravery, strength and modesty as a demand on the German language. He is concerned with placing German as a self-confident cultural and artistic language on an equal footing with Spanish, French and Italian. Another important component of Opitz's normative poetics consists in his proposal of a new metrical count consisting of a combination of alternation and accentuation. This is consistent with his view of German as a natural language, since according to Opitz's rules it was now possible for any native speaker with an average feeling for language to form correct verse. The

The ancient counting method cannot be transferred one-to-one to the German language and was therefore reserved only for Latin or Greek scholars.

At the same time, language lovers such as Philipp von Zesen and Paul Fleming were pushing ahead with the development of a unified German language, as it was still very fragmentary, quite in keeping with the confused political circumstances.

Together with the aesthetics of Martin Opitz, they formed the basis for Baroque German literature.

Characteristic are the thematic contradictions, which can also be found in the formal structure of the texts, whereby the motifs of *memento mori, carpe diem* and *vanitas* were particularly *prominent.* In this context, *carpe diem* and *memento mori are* a pair of opposites: on the one hand, the appellative *Nutze den Tag, reminiscent of* Epicurean teachings, and on the other, the fatalistic-resignative *Bedenke, dass du sterblich bist,* which contrasts with the former. Finally, *vanitas* focuses on the transience of all being, which also includes the nothingness of man. These motifs are especially reflected in poetry, as its formal conventions correspond strongly with antithesis and paradox. The most popular form, the sonnet after Petrarch, was written (following Opitz or the French model instead of the Petrarchic Endecasillabo [Eleven Silver]) in the Alexandrian, an iamb with six stresses and audible censorship after the third stress. In addition, the division of the sonnet into four- and three-line stanzas, the so-called quartets and tercets, creates a further tension that can also be

made fruitful in terms of content. A very good example is the following sonnet by Andreas Gryphius
from 1637 entitled *Es ist alles eitel*, reproduced
here in a modernized version:

"You see, wherever you look, only vanity on earth.
What this one builds today, that one tears down tomorrow:
Where now cities still stand, will be a meadow,
On which a shepherd's child will play with the flocks.

What now still blooms splendidly, shall soon be trampled.
What now so throbs and defies, tomorrow is ashes and bones,
Nothing is that eternal, no ore, no marble stone.
Now happiness laughs at us, soon the complaints thunder.

The glory of high deeds must vanish
like a dream.
Shall then the game of time, the light man, endure?
Alas! What is all this, what we consider delicious,

As a vile trifle, as a shadow, dust, and wind;
As a meadow-flower that cannot be found again. Nor
will a single man consider
what is eternal!"

Already in the first stanza it becomes clear how
virtuously the antithetical structure of the Alexandrian can be used. The main motif of *vanitas is*
revealed in the juxtaposition of the present and

the future, which predominates in the second two verses. The title-giving vanity is to be understood in its original literal sense as nothingness, which makes the recurrence to *vanitas* clearer.

In the second stanza Gryphius continues the thought, the caesura is still used as a mirror axis. Then, with the formal break of the sonnet, there is also a break in content, in that the poet makes more general, philosophical considerations and, on the one hand, propagates the inevitability of transience and, on the other hand, presents a fatalistic overcoming of the world as a solution for present suffering. The toils and burdens of earthly life can only be outweighed by the eternal after death, as the last verse makes clear.

Gryphius' Christian imprint is one way of dealing with the aforementioned motifs; another can be found, for example, in poems by Hoffmannswaldau, such as *Wo sind die Stunden, in* which a more secular approach - at least at first glance - is evident.

Epic poetry was a rather secondary genre in the Baroque period, but in 1668 a novel appeared that is still considered one of the most important

German-language works of all time. It was written by Hans Jakob Christoffel von Grimmelshausen, who was born in Hesse in 1622 and died eight years after the publication of his main work. During the Thirty Years' War he worked as a mercenary, and after the war he had various occupations. His literary activity probably began only 15 years before his death, as indicated by the publication dates of his works. *The abentheuerliche* Simplicissimus *Teutsch* or, abbreviated, *Simplicius Simplicissimus* is considered one of the first German adventure novels and the most important Baroque novel. The three-part plot has the main theme of the disillusionment of the naïve hero and is divided into the initiation, the journey through large parts of Germany, in the course of which Simplicius becomes acquainted with the society of his present, and finally the retrospective of the experiences in the course of his life.

As a child, the novel's hero must flee his father's farm when marauding gangs ravage the home. He runs into the forest and is taken in by a Christian hermit, who instructs him accordingly and teaches him to read and write. From him he also receives his nickname Simplicius. After some time, his mentor reveals to him that he will soon die. Shortly thereafter, Simplicius, whose real name is Melchior Sternfels von Fuchshaim, leaves the hermitage, but on his further journey he is again struck by war and returns to the hut of the hermit, who has left him a letter in which he teaches him the three basic pillars of a good way of life, which consist of self-knowledge, knowledge of the world, and constancy. After some entanglements, Simplicius arrives at the court of the Swedish governor in Hanau, who, it turns out, is related to him. There, however, disillusionment and alienation take place, as a result of which he falls from grace and is demoted to the status of fool. With the help of a priest, however, he remains true to his (Christian) ideals and continues his journey, escaping enemy soldiers again and again before joining the imperial forces as a jester before Magdeburg.

He flees from there again and finally lands in Soest, where, after the death of his master, he is now a private and gains fame and money as a hunter of Soest by committing misdeeds. When he challenges two soldiers to a duel, he is again captured, but after devising a battle-deciding ruse, he is released. After reaching Paris via Cologne and becoming rich twice, having been robbed in the meantime, he is again forced to go to war. After further trials and tribulations, he finally meets someone he met in the imperial forces. During a joint pilgrimage, he again loses a potential fortune when he renders worthless a stone given to him by the king of the water spirits, which can produce a healing spring, by placing it on the ground. He then retreats to a farm and, after some time, is captured there by camping soldiers and, by several coincidences, is sent once around the world. He finally lands on an island near Spain and writes down his account of his life, which makes it back to Germany through a Dutch sailor, ending the book.

This, mind you, brief summary of the contents shows how exuberant and sprawling baroque literature can sometimes be. Grimmelshausen's main character experiences everything and encounters everyone, and the entire novel is a milestone of German literature simply because of its joy in experimentation, which despite everything is bound to certain conventions of the time or the genre.

The Baroque, however, disappeared into oblivion shortly thereafter. The reason for this was the contempt shown for it by the Enlightenment and Sturm und Drang.

ENLIGHTENMENT & STURM UND DRANG

The rise of the bourgeoisie within the society of the estates and the improved educational opportunities also changed literature: the recipients were no longer limited to the nobility and a few educated and wealthy citizens, but the reading public began to expand. Religion lost importance, and with it the leitmotifs and Christian moral concepts that defined the Baroque. Of course, these continued to play a role, but a subordinate one. The clear expression and the closeness to life or practice of the material dealt with took the place of enigma and strongly pronounced imagery.

Poets such as Christian Fürchtegott Gellert, with his didactically conceived fables, and Johann Christoph Gottsched, whose 1730 *poetics Versuch einer critischen Dichtkunst vor die Deutschen (Attempt at a Critical Poetry for the Germans) had a* strong normative influence, were early representatives of an Enlightenment literature. The most important Enlightenment writer in the German language, however, was Gotthold Ephraim Lessing, whose most important drama *Nathan the Wise is an* impressive plea for tolerance and cultural understanding. The famous Ring Parable in particular, placed as a moral lesson at the center of the drama, is an impressive testimony to this. Lessing, in contrast to Gottsched, advocated a literature that was less rule-governed and acted more at eye level with the reader, which did not act in a lecturing manner, but rather achieved a catharsis-like effect in reminiscence of antiquity.

Not entirely insignificant in the course of the Enlightenment is the fact that Latin was also replaced by French as the lingua franca in the sciences. In addition, the language of philosophy changed to the respective national language, which made it accessible to broader masses of educated laymen. The masterminds of the Enlightenment, in Germany of course above all Immanuel Kant, had as their goal the liberation of man from his self-inflicted immaturity. In 1781, the Königsberg professor published his major work, representing a turning point in philosophy, the *Critique of Pure Reason, in* which he examined the possibilities of ontology as a science. In addition, three years later he declared the Horace quotation *sapere aude* to be the guiding principle of the Enlightenment, as which it has endured to this day.

Thus, while philosophy dealt with the theoretical background and discussed questions of principle, literature placed itself at the service of clear intellectual expression. But the rule-bound nature of literature was soon called into question by young poets who were to establish a literary movement of their own: that of Sturm und Drang.

The new generation set feeling as an equal standard alongside reason, and it was given even higher priority for text production itself. Imagination and ingenuity, emotion and genius joined the ideals of reason and clarity of mind to form the breeding ground for a new kind of texts. Johann Gottfried Herder's calls for recognition of popular poetry and his assumption that the Enlightenment had too long been arrogant toward the common people were positively received and internalized by fellow poets. The works of early Goethe and Schiller, for example, were written along his lines.

Both *Die Leiden des jungen Werther (The Sorrows of Young Werther)*, Goethe's epistolary novel about the unhappy protagonist in love of the same name, and Friedrich Schiller's *Die Räuber (The Robbers)*, at whose premiere in Mannheim in 1781 indescribable scenes unfolded, are impressive testimonies to the power and passion that the Sturm und Drang brought with it. With its proto-Romantic emphasis on emotion, this epoch represents a decisive turning point in the history of German literature, which until then had only sporadically brought the individual to the fore. Goethe and Schiller also published significant poems at this time, many of which have since become canonized and can be found in countless compilations of the most famous or popular German poems. In Schiller's case, the Ode *to Joy is* notable, which provided the text for the finale of Ludwig van Beethoven's 9th Symphony, later designated the European anthem. In Goethe's case, it is above all the poem *Willkommen und Abschied (Welcome and Farewell) that has* burned itself into the collective memory.

Both authors founded the epoch of Weimar Classicism, which ended the Sturm und Drang and focused unusually strongly on one geographical location as its center.

CLASSIC

The Classical period, often referred to as the *Weimar period,* can be divided into two periods: In the narrower sense, it refers to that of the intensive correspondence between Friedrich Schiller and Johann Wolfgang von Goethe, which began with the start of their exchange of letters in 1794 and ended with Schiller's death in 1805. If we take it further (and expand it to include the literary work of the authors Wieland and Herder, who were not directly connected with the two German national poets), we can date it between Goethe's first trip to Italy in 1786 and his death 46 years later. The important point of reference for this literary current was the German art historian Johann Joachim Winckelmann, who wrote two writings on Greek and Roman antiquity in the second half of the 18th century.

In his view, the quality of Western antiquity consisted in something that he tried to describe with the pair of terms *noble simplicity, silent greatness.* This statement, understood as a maxim by the classical poets, met the tendency of German literature to build bridges between the nobility and the bourgeoisie, which it had developed since the Enlightenment. Through various events, the four great poets moved to Weimar one after the other, the last to arrive in 1799 being Friedrich Schiller, who by this time was already linked to Goethe by an intimate friendship.

The most important keyword in relation to the literary creativity of the epoch is harmony or, expressed in processual terms, harmonization. Taking its cue from the ancient ideal, the unity of content and form became the most important goal, which meant a retreat after the expansive eras of the Enlightenment and the Sturm und Drang. This was also due, among other things, to the failure of the French Revolution, which was a disappointment for many artists, not only in literature, but also for composers such as Ludwig van Beethoven. In contrast to the turbulent times, the cultural program of the classical literati wanted to achieve a level education and aesthetic training of the citizens towards the enlightened and humanistic ideal. This is evident, for example, in Schiller's poem "Die Bürgschaft," from which you will read excerpts later in this book.

During the Classical period, a return to the ancient drama form can be observed, especially in Goethe and Schiller, whose three units of place, time, and action served both as models.

The metrical forms also approached a strictly regulated ideal, the most exquisite expressions of which can be found, among others, in Goethe's blank verse drama *Iphigenie auf Tauris*. Schiller, who often found his inspiration in historical material, wrote at this time, among others, The *Maid of Orleans, William Tell,* and his drama about Mary Stuart, heir to the Scottish throne. Wieland and

Herder, who were somewhat distanced from the Goethe/Schiller duo on a personal level, published many theoretical writings (Herder) and novels (Wieland) that operated on ancient material.

It may be considered contradictory that Goethe at this time continued to deal with his opus magnum *Faust*, the two parts of which appeared 24 years apart in 1808 and 1832. However, since this piece stands as a monolith in German literary history anyway, it is perhaps less surprising than it might seem that Goethe renounced his self-imposed antique ideals in *Faust*.

Because the Classical period was so thematically and spatially limited, it is clear that some important poets did not participate in it. The most important example of this is Heinrich von Kleist, who was held in low esteem by Goethe and whose poetic work cannot be classified as belonging either to the Classical period or to the burgeoning early Romantic period. Although he frequently takes up ancient material in his plays and also adheres to the stylistic guidelines formulated by Aristotle in his *Poetics*, Kleist is more interested in

the abysmal and extreme aspects of human existence.

At the same time that Schiller and Goethe were burying themselves in ancient material and Kleist was creating his elaborate stories and dramas away from literary life, a new literary movement was emerging that had certain points of connection to the Sturm und Drang, but nevertheless represented a major innovation: Romanticism.

ROMANTICISM

> "Romantic poetry is a progressive universal poetry. [...] Romantic poetry is still in the process of becoming; indeed, this is its very essence, that it can eternally only become, never be completed. It cannot be exhausted by any theory [...]."

This attempt at a Romantic definition of poetics comes from Friedrich Schlegel, one of the pioneers of German Romanticism as well as Romanticism in general. It already hints at the essential Romantic concerns, in particular the intended bringing into harmony of man and nature as well as soul and spirit, which is reflected in the concept of *progressive universal poetry*. Also noteworthy is the statement, reproduced in the second part of the quotation, that the "romantic poetry" cannot be completed. On the one hand, the processes of alienation between man and nature already felt on the threshold of the nineteenth century become clear here, since the desired union cannot be achieved; on the other hand, Schlegel explicitly opposes the primacy of man guided purely by reason by attributing to Romantic poetry that it cannot be theorized. This reveals the spirit of Romanticism as an explicit countermovement to the Enlightenment, flanked by the intellectual flights of fancy of Johann Gottlieb Fichte and Friedrich Wilhelm Schelling, that is, idealist philosophy.

Against the backdrop of the French Revolution, the Napoleonic turmoil of war, and finally the Congress of Vienna in 1815, an artistic movement unfolded that encompassed all artistic genres, from literature to music to painting, and was devoted to fantasy and the irrational, as enthusiastic about the mental abysses of man as it was about the Middle Ages as an idealized state of desire. Socially, this was accompanied by a rejection of bourgeois habits of life.

An important undercurrent is the so-called Black Romanticism, which deepened the already existing Romantic fascination with the morbid and uncanny and made it the main theme of their texts. Motifs such as the nightmare or that of the doppelganger, which enables a reflection of the self and thus already refers to Freud (in the interpretation of the doppelganger as a confrontation between the ego and its id), determined the texts of poets such as E. T. A. Hoffmann.

The latter can be considered the most important German representative of Black Romanticism; his works, such as *The Sandman* or *The Elixirs of the Devil,* also met with great approval abroad, especially in Russia and France, and influenced important poets such as Gogol, Dostoievski or Poe.

The most important genres of Romanticism were epic poetry and lyric poetry; drama found almost no use; it was felt to be too over-formed by ancient, rigid rules. Poems and stories were considered better suited to portraying emotions and thus following the Romantic ideal. The most frequently thematized emotion was longing, which one tried to capture in images corresponding to it. The following poem by Joseph von Eichendorff uses the famous thing symbol of the blue flower, which was first used by Novalis in his novel fragment *Heinrich von Ofterdingen:*

"I search for the blue flower,
I search and never find it,
I dream that in the flower
my good luck blossoms for
me.

I wander with my harp
through countries, cities and meadows,
If nowhere in the round to see the
blue flower.

I've been walking for a long time, I've
hoped for a long time, I've
trusted,
But oh, nowhere have I
seen the blue flower."

On the one hand, the blue flower is used in its meaning as a symbol of longing; on the other hand, however, Eichendorff reflects on the function of this stylistic device. The symbol of longing cannot be found, after all, and poetic processing alone does not cancel out the oppressive feeling.

In this way, he already points beyond the Romantic period, which was slowly coming to an end as the political situation in Germany became more unsettled again and something new was in the air, which was also processed in literature by authors such as Georg Büchner, particularly in the Vormärz period.

Heinrich Heine, whose poems and essayistic works made everyday language capable of art, is considered to have overcome Romanticism.

We skip the turbulent times surrounding the 1848 Revolution and move toward realism and naturalism.

REALISM/NATURALISM

Historically, realism owes its existence to a change of mood after the failed revolution. The liberal-minded bourgeoisie, which had made up the bulk of the revolutionaries, saw itself confronted with the shambles of idealism, the philosophical current that had started with Hegel and Fichte, after its demands had hardly been implemented.

Thus, also literarily, the will to contemplate the world as it is came to the center.

First of all, it is necessary to clarify some conceptual difficulties. Realism does not represent a clumsy reproduction of all events, but rather, under certain circumstances, assembles a new reality from sections of reality. Terms such as *bourgeois* or *poetic* realism already indicate the multifaceted interpretation of realism. The former seeks to depict, in addition to the material world, a moral reality that, subjected to its time, mostly emphasized the value of work and education and an assimilated life. Poetic realism, on the other hand, puts the working methods and literary techniques at the service of art, which should also be understood as such. It often combines a subjective narrative approach with the imitation of social reality.

Furthermore, realism can be divided into two decisive phases, the first of which was linked to Ludwig Feuerbach's religion philosophy, which built on mutual solidarity in the face of transcendental homelessness and saw man as God for man. Industrialization, initially received positively, reinforced this auto-emancipatory attitude.

However, with the increasing social problems and the development of evolutionary theories on the part of Alfred Russel Wallace and Charles Darwin, the optimistic basic mood gave way to a certain resignation, which saw man subjected to biological and social constraints from which he could not free himself.

German representatives of this pan-Western current were Theodor Storm, Adalbert Stifter, C. F. Meyer, Gottfried Keller, and, as the most important protagonist, Theodor Fontane, whose social novels *Irrungen, Wirrungen* (1888), *Frau Jenny Treibel* (1892), and *Effi Briest* (1895) decisively shaped poetic realism and completed it with *Effi Briest*.

While in realism the poetic exaggeration of reality and its purpose-bound representation were decisive, it became the goal of the naturalists to represent all facets of reality without omitting supposedly negative episodes. It was based on an understanding of science that assumed that everything could be explained, and this positivism was also transferred to the individual, who is bound to his conditions determined by social origin and heredity and acts in a predictable manner.

The writer Arno Holz identified the ideal type of naturalistic text in the formula *Art = Nature - x,* where *x* represents the artistic influence to be kept as small as possible. The literary movement, which lasted only a short time, formed as a reaction to the social problems caused by advancing industrialization and increasing urbanization. The German naturalists around Gerhart Hauptmann, Arno Holz, Frank Wedekind and Hedwig Dohm received inspiration from international models such as Émile Zola. The social question was often discussed and the reality of life of the workers was portrayed as accurately as possible (Gerhart Hauptmann's drama *Die Weber* is a good example of this). The numerous peculiarities of language were also reproduced without comment; in Hauptmann's most important drama, for example, the Silesian dialect and the sociolect of the weavers.

The style of naturalism is first and foremost the close connection to science, which poets try to reproduce in reality empirically correct and true to nature. In doing so, they use scientific methods themselves. The author as an artist recedes into the background; instead, he tries to proceed in a documentary manner, for which he gives up his individuality and subjectivity, at least in part. The poet appears as a literary scientist who views man in his current situation as the end result of his social or biological origins, and thus certainly refers to Karl Marx's socialism and the theory of evolution.

With the rapid waning of naturalism in Germany, brought about in part by the Socialist Laws passed in 1890 and the supposed solution to the social question they brought, many different literary currents began to spread that are commonly subsumed under the term *modernism.*

MODERN

In the following, we will deal with three main directions of modern literature at the turn of the century: the Fin de Siècle, which absorbed and artistically expressed the feeling of the times, and the styles of Impressionism and Expressionism, which were adjacent to it.

The fin de siècle, or end of the century, originated in the French-speaking world, but was quickly adapted as a description of an epoch for the whole of European culture. As an artistic current, it took up the contradictory feelings and impulses and gave them a voice. The end of the 19th century was marked by nationalism and tendencies toward demarcation, which brought with them an increasingly tense international situation. Fear of the future and confidence were mixed with a fatalistic mood of the end of time, which matched the general situation of the authors, who saw themselves subjected to the compulsion of the market.

Hugo von Hofmannsthal, who as a sixteen-year-old under the pseudonym Loris stirred up the Viennese literary scene, may well represent the dichotomy of the fin de siècle parabolically. In his early sonnet *Was ist die Welt? (What is the World?)*, he still sounds hopeful, seeing the titular world as "gifted with its own, unconsecrated beauty." A few years later, in the poem *Das Zeichen (The Sign)*, it sounds quite different:

> "And do you carry a sign,
> A crimson sign,
> It would also have to fade,
> It would go there too!"

Transience and resignation even in the face of hopeful rebellion contrast the youthful sonnet and clearly show the epoch-typical dichotomy within a person.

If we think of Impressionism, Claude Monet's water lilies immediately come to mind, of which he produced pictures in the most varied constellations of light and shadow. Otto F. Best draws the following line of connection to Impressionist painting in his book on Impressionism and Symbolism: "Similarly, literary Impressionism can be described as the art of personal momentary sensation: from the experience that things as they 'really' are cannot be reproduced artistically, the Impressionist takes up subjective impressions of sections of the world and shapes them - mostly in lyrical poems [...]".

This very accurate definition is true if we look at the most important works of the Impressionists, of which the most popular is certainly Marcel Proust's *research*. In the German-speaking world, Stefan George, whose most famous verse can almost be read as a guide to Impressionism ("Komm in den totgesagten park und schau"), and Eduard von Keyserling, among others, stood out.

As an epoch more strongly in the fin de siècle tradition, Expressionism stood for renewal and anti-nationalist commitment in literature. Poems increasingly dealt with the problems of the big city, and the texts no longer had only an occasional socially critical note.

Magazines such as *Brenner* found outlets for the literary productions of the Expressionists, who pursued an agenda of breaking free from social and historical shackles. The poem that acted as the initial spark of Expressionism was Jakob van Hoddis' *Weltende,* published in 1911. In numerous disruptive images, he depicts the fragmentation of modern metropolitan life in just eight lines.

Despite a clear direction of thrust, the broad field of Expressionism allowed for a high individual range. Georg Trakl was close to Symbolism with his enigmatic poems about the mythical and numinous, whose ciphers cannot be fully deciphered, while Gottfried Benn broke most radically with traditional notions of value and morality when he published *Morgue and Other Poems in 1912*, establishing an aesthetic of the ugly.

The metropolitan poetry as a dominant subcategory was founded in Expressionism and directly found its absolute climax. One example will be cited here in the form of Paul Boldt's *On the Terrace of Café Josty:*

"Potsdamer Platz in eternal roar
Glaciers all reverberating avalanches
The road clock: streetcars on iron rails
Automobiles and the human garbage.

People run across the asphalt,
Ant emsig, like lizards nimble.
Forehead and hands, blinking from thoughts,
swim like sunlight through dark forest.

Night rain envelops the square in a cave,

> Where bats, white, beat with wings
> And purple jellyfish lie - colored oils;
>
> They multiply, cut up by the wagons.-
> Splashes Berlin, the day's glittering nest,
> From the smoke of the night like pus from a plague."

The natural legories with which Boldt tries to capture the juggernaut of the big city in verse are, of course, in great contradiction to the technically overformed life of the city dweller. The meaninglessness and forlornness of the people are also hinted at, especially in the second stanza. Finally, the city is associated with disease and ruin, which allows the sonnet to stand as an archetypal example of expressionist poetry.

After the political tensions in Europe were unleashed in World War I, the first German democracy of the Weimar Republic gave birth to new literatures.

LITERATURE OF THE WEIMAR RE-PUBLIC

On November 9, 1918, the SPD politician Philipp Scheidemann proclaimed the Republic from the balcony of the Reichstag to forestall possible revolutionary ideas of the KPD and USPD, which had gathered around Karl Liebknecht and Rosa Luxemburg. After their assassination in 1919, which resulted in tumults and riots that were put down by imperial troops and the Freikorps, the Weimar Republic began to consolidate itself as a democratic republic. However, inflation, which was triggered by war funding and continued to rise after the war was lost, resulted in hyperinflation in 1923, the year of Hitler's coup.

Germany could no longer pay its reparations and wages were not adjusted to the rapidly rising costs. The threat of political unrest was only dispelled by a radical new beginning under Reich Chancellor Gustav Stresemann. The following years saw the so-called Golden Twenties, which were perceived as a cultural wedding, especially in the metropolis of Berlin. They ended in Black Thursday on the New York Stock Exchange and

Black Friday on the European stock exchanges, which triggered first inflation and then an even more fatal deflation favoring the eventual seizure of power by the National Socialists.

The most important literary direction of the young republic became the new objectivity, which was connected to naturalism, but had abandoned its idea of an all-encompassing positivistic science. It was the addition of a disillusioned awareness of political and social conditions that distinguished it from naturalism, which eliminated the poet. Practical approaches to life and the arming of the readership for modern society were important concerns of the authors, who often also spoke out decidedly in favor of democracy and tried to arouse a certain enthusiasm in their recipients as well. Poetry and versification played less of a role than the exact reproduction of observation, as Joseph Roth postulates in the preface to a novel: "It is no longer a question of 'writing poetry.' The important thing is what is observed."

The genre of the novel, which was striving to flourish once again, enjoyed great popularity among both writers and the reading public and was closely linked to the reality of life in the Weimar Republic, which was portrayed as faithfully as possible in accordance with the style of its era.

The statement *form follows function, which is* still popular today, could well have come from the Weimar Republic, because the content was more important to the poets than the formal prettification of their works. Moreover, characters were often characterized as types rather than as independent individuals, in order to simplify the representation of a social class rather than the personal situation. By far the most important novel of the New Objectivity, transcending it as it were, is *Berlin Alexanderplatz* by Alfred Döblin from 1929, which depicts the life of Franz Biberkopf.

Analogous to its epic poetry, the epoch also developed an independent lyric poetry, which was characterized by a novel use of language as well as the connection of the trivial and the comical with high culture. Kurt Tucholsky in particular, and Erich Kästner, who was unjustly known primarily as a children's book author, drove this style of poetry, also known as Gebrauchslyrik, by combining everyday scenes with subtle deeper meaning, often expressed in subtle irony or sheer comedy. Another important representative of this style is the poet Mascha Kaléko, in whose poetry the pain that is more subtle or overplayed in the aforementioned authors is more apparent.

After the introduction of women's suffrage in 1919, more and more women also celebrated success in literature. Two of the most important female authors during the Weimar Republic were Vicky Baum and Irmgard Keun. The former achieved great financial success with her novels, which oscillated between entertaining and upscale literature, but was always eyed with suspicion by literary critics. Although she was considered to have certain literary qualities, she was criticized for being too close to kitsch and triviality. Baum herself, who was posthumously accused of homophobic and misogynistic tendencies, knew how to place herself self-deprecatingly and spoke of herself as a "first-class second-rate writer.

The situation was somewhat different for Irmgard Keun: although her first two novels *Gilgi, eine von uns* and *Das kunstseidene Mädchen* were financial successes at the end of the Weimar Republic and were also well received by critics, Keun's situation at the time of the Nazi regime was more difficult than that of Vicky Baum, who remained in the USA after the film adaptation of her world bestseller *Menschen im Hotel.*

Irmgard Keun first emigrated to Belgium and the Netherlands, where she continued to publish in exile publishing houses before returning illegally to Germany. After the end of the Second World War, however, she found no connection to the literary scene in West Germany and became impoverished. Only shortly before her death were she and her work rediscovered. In recent years, large parts of her work were published as paperbacks by Ullstein Verlag, and literary scholars recognized not only the great entertainment value of Keun's novels but also their literary significance.

The authors who remained in Germany created little of significance at the time of National Socialism - with the possible exception of Benn and Kästner - which is why in the next chapter we will look at German-language exile literature and

illuminate what a drastic loss for German literature the forced exile of so many important authors
meant.

EXILE LITERATURE

After the National Socialists seized power in 1933,
many writers initially tried to find their way under
the changed political auspices. This plot changed
for most in the course of the book burnings, in
which the works of non-Aryan and so-called de-
generate artists went up in flames on May 10. This
was followed by the emigration to other European
and international countries of many authors who
were endangered because of their origins or political views. However, when the Nazis began to an-
nex territories, those who had fled there were
once again faced with the question of where they
could escape to. Sometimes draconian entry regu-
lations made escape even more difficult. The situation deteriorated further with the start of World
War II in 1939, when poets who had thought
themselves safe in France, Belgium, or the Netherlands had to quickly try to get to Great Britain or

the United States. Anne Frank is the most famous example of the fact that even those who had emigrated were caught and deported in the course of the Nazi wars of conquest.

Even after the end of the war, there was great uncertainty among the emigrants. Some of them returned to Germany, but they were not met with only enthusiasm. The young post-war Germany resented their intellectual struggle against the Nazi regime. The authors who remained abroad continued to face the familiar problems that did not abate after the Allied victory.

The possibilities for publishing their texts were limited for the approximately 1500 exiled writers because there were hardly any magazines for German-language literature. With the disintegration of the heterogeneous German literary scene and its diaspora, the institutions and platforms that the emigrants had previously been able to use were also lost. Moreover, many had only managed to escape with forged papers and were denied German citizenship after their exile.

Thus, they had to submit to the dictates of the respective immigration authorities and were constantly threatened with the revocation of their visas or the end of their toleration. In addition to the permanent fear of deportation and the clutches of the Nazi regime, many of the emigrants were seen by the respective population as potential informers and were therefore met with hostility. On a material level, all of this resulted in the fact that only very few exiled poets were able to secure their livelihood with their writing, and for many of them, major financial problems arose. Emotionally, the time was no less demanding; psychological trauma was very common and a number of artists who had emigrated from Germany committed suicide.

Due to the wide spatial distribution alone, it would hardly have been possible for the exiles to find a common style with a corresponding poetic basis. However, there was hardly any interest in this anyway. In their literary work, most of them followed the route they had already taken before 1933.

The novel was by far the most popular form of literary expression, in large part because it had greater sales prospects than other types of texts and accommodated the international readership with its reading habits. They often addressed the Third Reich, either depicting its prehistory and conditionality or thinking it through to its catastrophic end. Another way of dealing with events in Germany was the historical novel, in which certain historical events were analogized to those of the Third Reich. Another variation of this type of novel was the actual concentration on historical material, which was said to have escapist tendencies. Also worthy of mention is the autobiographical novel, in which one's own life story was illuminated against the background of the epochal events of the time. An outstanding example of this is Stefan Zweig's last completed work, *Die Welt von Gestern*.

Drama and poetry hardly played a role for exile literature, which was much connected with practical problems. Basically, however, it can be said for these two genres that they were dominated by poets who had already achieved prominence in the Weimar Republic.

Many of the exiled writers sought ways to express their rejection of the Nazi regime in an activist way as well. The greatest attempt was made by the most famous of them, Thomas Mann. In 55 radio speeches under the title "Deutsche Hörer" (German Listeners), he sent appeals for resistance and reflections on current events to the Germans via the BBC. The five- to eight-minute episodes were sent via longwave, so it was possible to listen to them with the Volksempfänger. Even if their influence cannot be taxed, they were not entirely without effect, as Hitler's denigration of Mann shows.

Since the founding of the Federal Republic and the GDR in 1949, a lot has happened in literature that we are still too close to historically to be able to classify more closely. That is why the chapter "Contemporary Literature" covers as much as possible of what has happened literarily in Germany in recent decades.

The first genre to establish itself in Germany after World War II was the so-called Trümmerliteratur, which passed into postwar literature. Trümmerliteratur was characterized by a laconic use of language, the purpose of which was to free German from National Socialist ballast. The authors' required closeness to life was rooted in the strong need for security and practical solutions that defined the immediate postwar period.

Postwar literature, in turn, is a more chronologically oriented description of literary currents and encompasses various forms and stylistic ideas. While the literature of the GDR focused largely on carrying the new socialist state, various forms of dealing with the legacy of the previous decades emerged in West Germany. Böll's socially critical social panoramas stood alongside the hermetic poetry of a Paul Celan.

In the 1950s, Eugen Gomringer laid *the* foundation for concrete poetry in the German-speaking world with his text *vom vers zur konstellation*. Its goal is to detach the word from its hermeneutic content and to let it function as a concrete object in its phonetic as well as visual design. Playing with the elements of meaning is just as much a part of concrete poetry as the arrangement of word or letter clusters. In all casualness, the poetic creations stimulate debate about meaning and perception, as the following short text by Eugen Gomringer shows:

silence silence silence
silence silence silence
silence silence
silence silence silence
silence silence silence

In this poem, the meaning of the term can be obtained on the one hand through the knowledge of the word, but on the other hand also through the purely visual element of the blank space.

Concrete poetry was particularly widespread in the poetry circles of the Vienna Group and the Stuttgart School. In addition to Gomringer, Ernst Jandl and Helmut Heißenbüttel are among its most important representatives.

After the post-war period had been overcome and German guilt had begun to be acknowledged,

a literature developed in the seventies that the renowned critic Marcel Reich-Ranicki described as a
new subjectivity, which focused on the depiction
of personal dreams and private problems. This
was in contrast to the politically and socially committed literature of the late 1960s, which was also
predominant, but also to a poetics committed to
literary experimentation that drew its inspiration
from classical modernism. Although social criticism was voiced, it was always embedded in personal experience. This development blossomed,
for example, with Christa Wolf's *Nachdenken über
Christa T.*, which appeared in 1968. Self-recogni-
tion and a look into one's own psyche were the
defining approaches of the new-subjective authors.

"Well, it starts with me standing at Fisch-Gosch in
List on Sylt and drinking a Jever from the bottle.
Fisch-Gosch is a fish stall that is so famous because it is the northernmost fish stall in Germany.
It's at the top tip of Sylt, right by the sea, and you
think there's a border coming up, but in reality
there's just a fish stall. So I stand there at Gosch

and drink a Jever. Because it's a bit cold and a westerly wind is blowing, I'm wearing a Barbour jacket with a lining. In the meantime, I eat the second portion of scampi with garlic sauce, although I was already sick after the first. The sky is blue. Now and then a thick cloud pushes itself in front of the sun. Earlier I met Karin again. We still know each other from Salem, although we didn't talk back then, and I've seen her a few times at Traxx in Hamburg and at P1 in Munich."

This is the beginning of Christian Kracht's novel *Faserland*, published in 1995 and considered a milestone of pop literature. This consists in part of the pop-cultural references captured in its name, but on closer examination it cannot be said to be without pretensions. Roughly speaking, pop literature is any literature that emerges under the market mechanisms of late capitalism and addresses its present accordingly.

And today? Today, many things are happening in literature that can only be summarized as currents in retrospective. Whether the role of women and mothers is addressed, as in the work of

Anke Stelling, whether experiences of discrimination are linked with social criticism, as in the work of Deniz Ohde, whether the country and one's own life are addressed with a new kind of wit, as in the novels of Sasa Stanisic, or whether the focus is on the subtlety of language and the poetic experience of reality, as in the work of Peter Handke: the diversity of contemporary German literature is great.

German Poets, German Thinkers: Three Examples

It is actually an impossible undertaking to single out just three of the plethora of German intellectual greats. On the other hand, focusing more closely on Friedrich Schiller, Rainer Maria Rilke, and Daniel Kehlmann allows us to present their complete works and provide you with a better overview of the entire oeuvre of the three chosen authors. After a presentation of the circumstances of the three authors' lives, each will be discussed in more detail, with different emphases.

FRIEDRICH SCHILLER

The Marbach poet was born on November 10, 1759, the son of an officer. After two moves, Schiller became a member of the Latin school in Ludwigsburg. At the Karlsschule, which he was forced to join at the duke's behest, he devoted himself to the study of law while he and his classmates were under military drill. Later he changed his field and turned to medicine, at which time he also began to study literature more intensively. After several attempts at a dissertation, Schiller was finally employed as a military doctor with a doctorate in a regiment of the Württemberg army, but was never entirely satisfied with this post.

In 1781, Schiller completed his play *Die Räuber (The Robbers),* begun a few years earlier, which premiered in Mannheim a year later. Due to various transgressions of Schiller's rules and political squabbles, the conflict between him and the duke came to a head until Schiller was forced to flee

Stuttgart because he had been forbidden to write non-medically. This marked the beginning of years of uncertainty for him. He found shelter in a Thuringian village and continued his writing activities. After following a call to Mannheim as a theater poet in 1784, he had to move on a year later and found himself in the area around Leipzig and Dresden in 1785, where he stayed until 1788.

Here he finalized his *Don Karlos* and wrote the Ode *to Joy* before being appointed associate professor at the University of Jena in 1789. His precarious financial situation improved and he married Charlotte von Lengsfeld. Shortly after the wedding, however, he fell seriously ill, probably with tuberculosis, from which he did not recover until the end of his life. As far as his work was concerned, the last ten years of his life were the most fruitful, which was also due to his close friendship with Goethe. Schiller moved with his family to Weimar in 1799, where he died in 1805 in his mid-forties after a serious illness.

Let us first turn to Schiller's poetry, which was already held in low esteem by his contemporaries in comparison to Goethe. The critics' reproach was that Schiller was too anxious to capture philosophical and moral statements in lyrical form, and in doing so all too often drifted into the banal and trivial. This may be true for individual poems, but there are equally outstanding examples that confirm Schiller's genius and his rank as a poet. One of these is the ballad *Die Bürgschaft*, whose first stanza is testimony to how skillfully Schiller knew how to handle lyrical forms:

"To Dionys, the tyrant,

Damon crept,

the dagger in his garment:

Him the henchmen beat in bonds,

'What did you want with the dagger? Speak!'

The rageful man answered him darkly:

'To free the city from the tyrant!

' 'You shall regret that on the cross.'"

The exposition is completed with this first stanza, the hero of the ballad has been introduced to the readers and his fate is also known to us. As the plot progresses, Damon asks the tyrant for time to marry off his sister, leaving him his best friend as a guarantor, who must die in his place if he returns too late. The ruler agrees and Damon is on his way back in time to free his friend, but all sorts of adversities stand in his way: a change in the weather and thieves cause multiple delays. Here, Schiller's intended moral of unconditional loyalty as an ideal is clearly evident, but it does not seem heavy-handed or overly pathetic, which is a credit to Schiller's style. Damon finally manages to arrive on time, and the king, impressed by the friendship of the two, asks him to accept him as a friend as well.

However, the most important for German literature were undoubtedly Schiller's dramas, the most famous of which are *William Tell, Cabal and Love* and *The Robbers*.

Friedrich Schiller, with his perfectly formed verse in poetry and drama, is an author that each and every one of you should discover for yourselves.

When one hears the name of this Austrian poet, his best-known poems *Der Panther* and *Herbsttag* first come to mind, but the literary range of one of the most important poets of the modern era includes not only his poems but also stories, letters, texts on aesthetics, and a novel.

Rilke was born on the fourth of December 1875 in Bohemia, which was then part of Austria-Hungary.

He lived an unhappy childhood in Prague, marked by his father's professional failure and his mother's grief over the early death of his older sister. The mother could not get over the loss and pushed Rilke into the role of his sister.

After attending elementary school, Rilke transferred to a military school in Austria in 1886, but it was contrary to his talents and preferences, so he left it after six years and attended a commercial academy. After being expelled from school for a love affair, he prepared for the Austrian equivalent of the Abitur, the Matura, until 1895. After passing his final exams, he began studying in his hometown before moving to Munich a year later to attend the renowned Ludwig Maximilian University. A key encounter for Rilke was to be his meeting in 1897 with Lou Andreas-Salomé, fourteen years his senior, with whom he fell in love and on whose advice he changed his first name from René to Rainer. He was in a relationship with her for three years, but she remained an eminently important companion until his death. After Rilke followed Andreas-Salomé to Berlin, he made several trips, first alone to Italy and Worpswede, then in 1899 and 1900 to Russia with the Andreas-Salomé couple. On his first trip, he met Lev Tolstoy in Moscow, and on the second, by chance, the important poet Boris Pasternak.

After separating from Lou Andreas-Salomé, he married Clara Westhoff in 1901, but soon after the birth of his daughter he gave up family life and moved to Paris. He was permanently in a financially precarious situation, but this was accompanied by formative influences and stimuli that made Paris his second home.

Rilke found a new publisher in Anton Kippenberger of Insel-Verlag, for whom he became the most important contemporary author. After completing his only novel, *Die Aufzeichnungen des Malte Laurids Brigge (The Notes of Malte Laurids Brigge)*, in 1910, he entered a writing crisis that, although he began his groundbreaking *Duino Elegies*, was exacerbated by the outbreak of World War I and Rilke's induction into military service in 1916.

In 1919 Rilke traveled from Munich to Switzerland with the desire to continue work on his elegies. In Zurich he met Nanny Wunderly-Volkart, who supported him patronically and through whose cousin the residence Rilke found after two years was made available to the poet free of charge. Here he finally completed the *Duino Elegies* and the *Sonnets to Orpheus* within a short time in 1922, which represent a high point of his creative work.

From 1923 on, Rilke's health deteriorated visibly, which is why he went to a sanatorium several times and also tried to counteract his indisposition by moving to Paris for a short time. In the time until his death at the end of 1926, he still wrote a few poems and works in French that stood on their own. Rainer Maria Rilke was buried on the second of January 1927 near his last residence in Switzerland.

Rilke's work is strongly influenced by the philosophical reflections of Arthur Schopenhauer and Friedrich Nietzsche, whom he received early on. After a trip to the Orient, Rilke also became increasingly interested in Islam, while criticizing Christianity's lack of reference to this world. He can be seen as a representative of the transcendental insofar as he rejects a purely positivistic faith in science. On the other hand, a deep skepticism is inscribed in him, as can already be seen from the first line of the first of the Duino Elegies:

> "Who then, when I cried out, heard me out of the orders of angels?"

Overall, Rilke is rightly considered one of the most important German poets of the 20th century, whose *Letters to a Young Poet* and poems have received worldwide reception.

The last author worth reading, Daniel Kehlmann, was born in Munich on January 13, 1975. He is presented on the basis of his works, which produce a very unique, literary journey of development.

In 1997, Daniel Kehlmann entered the literary stage with his debut work *Beerholms Vorstellung*. The then twenty-two-year-old was thoroughly praised by the feuilleton, but there were complaints about an alleged lack of sovereignty and stylistic confidence. Kehlmann narrated the fictional biography of Arthur Beerholm, a magician who reflects on his life and turns as a narrative figure to a mysterious woman who remains strangely out of focus. An interesting introduction to Kehlmann's work.

He followed his debut novel in 1998 with the story collection *Under the Sun*, whose eight stories focus on man's longing for transcendence of existence. The strongest stories in the volume are *Pyr*, which is about a fire-setting television electrician, *Töten*, and the eponymous short story *Unter der Sonne*, but the other contributions to the volume are also evidence of Kehlmann's high literary level.

After the 1999 novel *Mahler's Time*, Daniel Kehlmann published the novella *Der fernste Ort (The Farthest Place)* with Suhrkamp in 2001, in which the protagonist Julian attempts to escape his previous life, which is depicted in flashbacks. Thematically, there are links to *Unter der Sonne (Under the Sun)*, and the author continues the magical realism he has cultivated since his debut. At the time, literary critics failed to recognize the ambivalent double structure of the novella, as Kehlmann himself noted in later works of popular literature.

His third novel, *Ich und Kaminski (I and Kaminski)*, *was* published in 2003 and is one of the best novels in contemporary German literature, a terrific comic comedy centered around Sebastian Zöllner, a self-aggrandizing art historian who wants to boost his career by writing a biography of Manuel Kaminski, a famous painter. In the course of his acquaintance with Kaminski, however, his cluelessness is revealed, contradicting his self-statements.

A delightfully entertaining and literarily sophisticated treat.

Just two years later, Kehlmann launched his most successful novel, the historical fiction *The Measurement of the World, about the* two German universal geniuses Alexander von Humboldt and Carl Friedrich Gauss. The stylistic peculiarity of this world bestseller is the dialogue kept in the subjunctive, which is rendered throughout as indirect speech and gives the book its own comic quality.

In 2007, he published *Ruhm - Ein Roman in neun Geschichten,* arguably his best work. Kehlmann's skillful postmodern play with reality and fiction, in which the characters all connect in certain ways through the concept of fame, is a milestone in German literature. Kehlmann succeeds in subtly linking the various episodes and thus formally mirroring the world of the Internet. In its partial mystery, the book is reminiscent of films like Quentin Tarantino's *Pulp Fiction.*

In *F* from 2013, the poet once again devotes himself to the world of art, but this is only one part among several within a familial web. Fate, Latin *fatum,* plays just as large a role as the partial indistinguishability of fact and fiction. The book was on the longlist for the German Book Prize.

2017 saw the publication of Kehlmann's latest novel to date, entitled *Tyll, which sets the* character of Till Eulenspiegel in the time of the Thirty Years' War. In a renewed play with truth and fiction, historically authenticated characters are introduced, such as the church scholar Athanasius Kircher, who puts Tyll's father on trial as a witch because of his knowledge of magic, or the poet Paul Fleming, one of the pioneers of New High German lyric poetry. The position of the church is ironized, for example, in that the Catholic witch trial leaders Kircher and Tesimond condemn superstition as a sin and a sign of witchcraft in accordance with doctrine, but make use of it themselves. In one scene of the novel, even a quoted magic square helps to find a way out of a predicament.

Daniel Kehlmann is undoubtedly an important contemporary writer whose multifaceted novels wonderfully combine reading pleasure and literary ambition.

From the Roots into the Future - An Outlook

"We ourselves stand disappointed and look aghast/ the curtain closed and all questions open." This sentence from the epilogue of Bertolt Brecht's play *The Good Man of Sezuan* can also be applied to the outlook for the future of German literature. What will happen in the future, we do not know. Will the postmodern tendencies continue and culminate in an avant-garde that loses sight of its

reading public? Will there be a literary conserva-
tism that resists technological developments and
possibly wistfully evokes the ideal world of y-
esterday? Or will entirely new literatures emerge,
carried by generations that have been socialized
with social media from the very beginning? All
that remains is for us to wait and read on, to enjoy
the new literary delights that appear and to redis-
cover the classic works. This effort is in no way in
vain, because, to paraphrase an apt phrase by So-
viet filmmaker Andrei Tarkovsky: Reading en-
sures that we not only look, but see.

www.ingramcontent.com/pod-product-compliance
Lightning Source LLC
Chambersburg PA
CBHW022058150726
47990CB00003B/1142